The Bruegel

Catherine de Duve

In collaboration with the Museums of Fine Arts
in Belgium

Pieter Bruegel
and his sons

In the days

Mark the items
painted by Bruegel

# of Bruegel

in the 16th century

Look at the world in Bruegel's day.
It's the Renaissance! Intellectuals are
fascinated by the literature of the ancient Greeks and
Romans. These intellectuals are known as the humanists!
Books are being printed for the first time. Trade and
art are developing as new continents are discovered.
In the holds of their ships, explorers are bringing
back plants, spices, gold and vegetables – things that
were previously unknown.

Bruegel i

Pieter Bruegel is a famous Flemish painter of the Renaissance.
He learned his craft in Antwerp, in the workshop of Master Pieter Coeck. In the 16th century, thanks to its port, Antwerp was one of the wealthiest cities in the world. Merchants, bankers, intellectuals and artists from all over the world were drawn to it.

*Pieter Bruegel the Elder
(around 1525-1569)*

Study the painting

A building site
with a crane

Stonemasons

Old houses

The port along the
river

The painter

Bruegel has a wooden panel prepared in his workshop.

Before painting:

1 Wooden panel

Oak planks joined together

2 Layer of white primer

Mixture of chalk and animal glue made from rabbit skins or fish bones

5 Applying the colours

Pigments come from nature: stones, plants or animal skins, ground to powder.

The colour is a mixture of pigments blended with siccative oil (which makes the paint dry) and volatile turpentine (which evaporates)

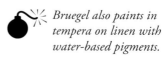 *Bruegel also paints in tempera on linen with water-based pigments.*

Look at how an oil painting
is made

Now painting can begin:

3 Imprimatura

Fine layer of translucent
ochre oil paint

4 Preparatory drawing

Sketch with a pen and ink
or charcoal

From stone to paint

Stone	Medium	Green pigment		Green paint

| Malachite, a green stone from Africa | Oil + turpentine | Grinding the stone into powder | | Mix the green pigment with the medium |

The Grea

The young Bruegel set out on his journey in 1552.
He travelled to southern Italy and drew the sea and the ships.
He crossed the Alps, often stopping to draw the mountains and valleys.
Bruegel is one of the first artists from the Low Countries to paint
landscapes based on sketches he made on his travels.

What a wonderful landscape!
But what is a Northern peasant doing working his field on the shores
of a Southern Sea? The painter is having fun mixing
times and places. The painting tells the story of Icarus, a hero from
Greek mythology.

*Mythology: People of Antiquity thought up fantastic stories – myths – to explain the world
and natural phenomena like lightening and earthquakes.*

The fall of Icarus

One day the King of Crete gets really angry with his architect Daedalus.

To punish him, he imprisons him and his son Icarus in a labyrinth.

The ingenious Daedalus finds a way to escape. He makes wings out of feathers and wax.

Father and son then fly off, across the sea.

Overwhelmed with joy at being free again, Icarus forgets all about his father's advice and flies too near the sun. The heat melts the wax… and he falls!

 Find Icarus in the painted landscape

What about you?
How would you draw the myth of Icarus?

W hen he came back to Antwerp, Bruegel worked for the famous publisher of engravings, Jerome Cock. This merchant's shop was called "The Four Winds", and it was a meeting place for artists, intellectuals and humanists. Bruegel received orders for drawings from which engravings would be made.

Alchemy is a science which – in the greatest secrecy – tries to discover the "philosopher's stone", the "magic" substance from which anything else can be made! Some alchemists believe that it can be found by melting down metals. Others hope to turn base metals into gold so they can get rich easily.

Colour the engraved story of the unlucky alchemist

 A poor woman shakes her empty purse into her hand – not a single penny!

 Her husband is ready to melt down their last coin in the hope of transforming it into gold.

 A grimacing fool in a cap is working the bellows.

 A wise man is pointing to the German word "Alghe mist" – "everything has failed" – in his book of magic spells.

 The children are being silly.

 The ruined family is begging for shelter at a poorhouse.

 How many cooking-pots has Bruegel drawn?

Study the alchemist's instruments and find them in the engraving Write the name under the correct picture

1. Book of magic spells
2. Athanor, a furnace in which fire burns forever
3. Alembic, distilling apparatus
4. Crucible, a pot in which metals are melted
5. Scales
6. Hourglass
7. Phial
8. Bellows

5

6

1

4

8

2

At the shop called "The Four Winds", Bruegel discovered the fantastic world of his older fellow-painter, Hieronymus Bosch. Fascinated, Bruegel was inspired by his work. Just judge for yourself !

Hieronymus Bosch

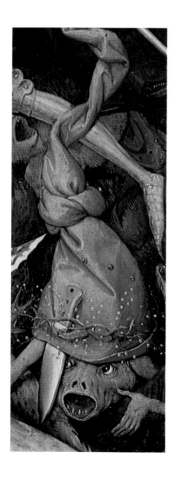

Pieter Bruegel

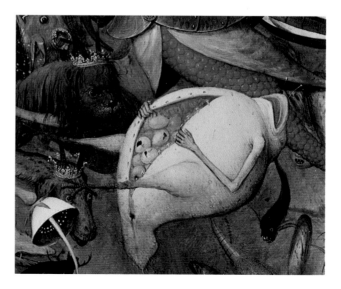

Draw a monster
like the ones Bruegel drew

Words an

Bruegel is very wise. He likes to warn people against
excess and illustrates popular Flemish words of advice or expressions,
known as proverbs, sayings or maxims.

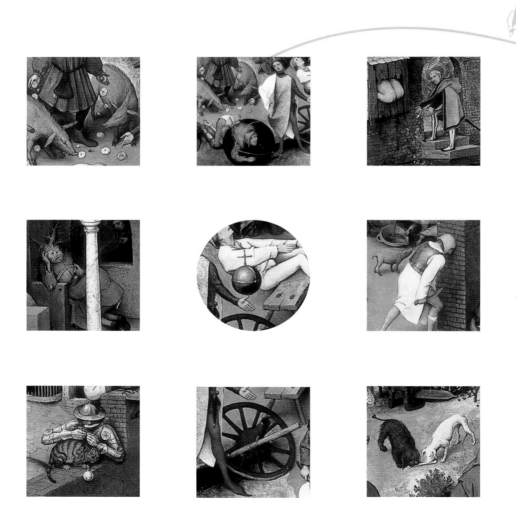

Learn the proverbs Bruegel illustrated and link them to the pictures. You can use them in the following situations:

When someone wants to get on in the world he'll find that...

to rise in the world you sometimes have to stoop first

When you talk to someone who is likely to repeat everything you say, you are...

confessing to the devil

When you're equipped against the cold from head to toe in mittens, coat, gloves, hat, cagoule, anorak…, then you are…

armed to the teeth

when you can't find a solution to your problem, you are…

banging your head against a brick wall

When you can persuade other people to do silly things, you can…

twist the world around your thumb

When you and a friend are arguing over the last sweet, we say…

two dogs rarely agree over a bone

When you spend a lot of money on useless things, you are…

throwing money out the window

When you give your dog the best chocolate cake in the world, you are …

casting pearls before swine

When somebody stops you from carrying out your plans, he is…

putting a spoke in your wheel

 Do you know a proverb? Write it here

Children'

People are more interested in children during the Renaissance.
The author Rabelais tells the story of the giant Gargantua's childhood,
while Bruegel paints lots of children's games in a single painting.
Can you count how many?

Circle the children
who are playing

blindman's bluff, leapfrog, a wedding, a baptism,
a procession, picking up a knife with their teeth,
a horseback duel, dancing
the farandole, with hoops,
on a hobbyhorse,
with skittles,
with soap bubbles,
boule...

Tripping up.
Look — the loser has been
given a forfeit. He has to walk
between two rows of sticking
out legs without tripping up.

Can you see him?

T O

What were toys made of in Bruegel's day?
The details from the painting below will help you:
Small bones: small pig bones coloured with onion juice
Balloon: a ball made of the intestines of cows, sheep or pigs
Red paint: ground red bricks
Boule: terracotta
The doll: rags
Sleigh: the skull of a bull or a cow
Ice-skates: wooden boards

Toys have a history:
Shepherds on the plains spent their days on tall stilts
so they could see their flock a long way off.
They used short stilts to cross swamps.
Rattles were used to warn people lepers were coming.

You can also make a toy
with things you can find and
recycle

Car

It is the day the "world is turned upside down".

On this day everything is allowed: gluttony, processions, singing, shouting, dancing, masks, dressing up, drinking, farces, games, begging, breaking things…

Everyone rejoices because spring is coming.

Children are kings. Look at the little King of the Carnival with his paper crown.

Father Winter is burnt.

People having fun playing break-the-pot.

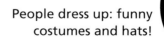

People dress up: funny costumes and hats!

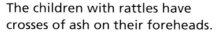

The children with rattles have crosses of ash on their foreheads.

 This is a Christian tradition which announces the first day of Lent and reminds us that we will all return to ashes.

 What day is this? Shrove Tuesday or Ash Wednesday?

Yum yum, here is Bruegel's secret waffle recipe!

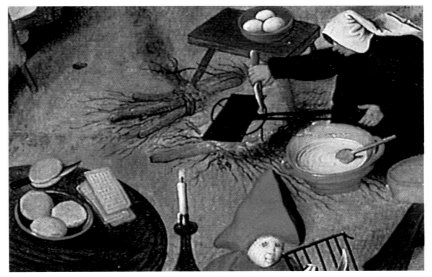

Prepare the equipment and the ingredients:

A waffle iron, a large bowl, a whisk, a small pan and a ladle.

3 eggs, 250 g of flour, 175 g of caster sugar, 15 g of yeast, 25 cl of beer
(a small bottle), 1 pinch of salt and 125 g of butter.

Put all the ingredients except the butter into a large bowl.
Beat it all together with a whisk till you have a smooth batter.

Leave the batter to rest for half an hour. Then put 125 g of butter in a small pan.
Melt it without burning it and add the melted butter to the batter just before
you are ready to make your waffles.
Pour a soup spoon of the batter onto the lightly oiled waffle iron
and close the waffle iron.

Enjoy your meal!

 What game are the gluttons
playing with the dice?

There is a party in the village! A wedding is being celebrated: processions, a religious ceremony, a banquet, music, dancing and beer for everyone! Bruegel, the townsman, is dressed as a peasant. He has slipped in amongst the guests so he can observe them discretely and describe them in his next paintings. When he got back to his workshop, he painted the joyous meal from memory!

After the banquet, it's time to dance!
Tomorrow, the young bride will wear a veil or a bun like all the other married women.

Study the painting and answer the questions:

Where is the bride?

The crown and canopy hung on the wall will help you to find her.

 What is special about her, compared to the other ladies at the banquet?

Where is the bridegroom?

The tradition was for the bridegroom to serve the guests.

Draw a bride you might see today

Where are the mystery guests?

There are three mystery guests among the peasants. Who are they ? Can you find them ?

Circle the answers

Where does the wedding meal take place?
inn - castle - barn - church

What are the guests drinking?
wine - beer - barley beer - champagne - lemonade

What are the guests eating?
pancakes - gruel - waterzooi - mashed potatoes

What instruments are the musicians playing?
Pan pipes - accordion - bagpipes - harmonica

Dancing

In Bruegel's day, everyone wears a hat.
There are hats for all tastes: felt berets, hats made of straw or the bark
of lime trees, wimples made of cloth, hats with feathers… Which one
would you choose to dance
at a wedding?

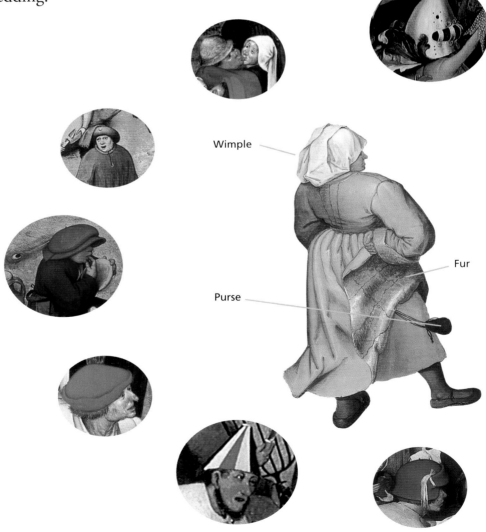

Wimple

Fur

Purse

In this dance of hats, find the intruders that don't belong to Bruegel's time

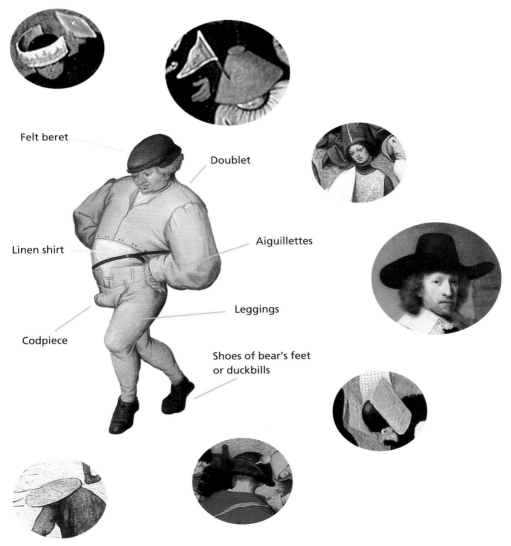

Felt beret

Doublet

Linen shirt

Aiguillettes

Codpiece

Leggings

Shoes of bear's feet or duckbills

Bruegel painted many winter landscapes towards the end
of his life. At this time, village life was governed by the rhythm
of the seasons. Winter laid its blanket of ice and snow over the village.
The fields lie dormant until the arrival of spring.
While the villagers are having fun on the frozen river the birds search for
food… but watch out for the trap!

Complete the
landscape

From Bruege

A family of painters.
In 1563, Bruegel married Mayken Coeck, the daughter of his Master.
They settled in Brussels and had two sons, Pieter the Younger
and Jan. Pieter Bruegel the Elder died whilst his sons were still young.

Pieter

Pieter Bruegel the Younger
ran a renowned
workshop.

As photography
had not yet been
invented, he
specialised in
making copies
of his father's
paintings.

These copies were
greatly valued
at the time.

to BruegHel

They learned their craft with their grandmother, who was also a painter. A new generation of great artists was born.

A letter has been added to Pieter and Jan's surname. Which one?

Jan

Jan, the youngest son of Bruegel, was born in 1568. He painted still-lifes, flowers, fruit, jewellery, landscapes and gardens of paradise.

He was called "Velvet Brueghel" because of the delicacy of his paintings.

Find these flowers in the painting

Cornflower, white peony, rose, blue iris, white tulip , hyacinth, daffodil, carnation…

Everyone would like to have a Bruegel at home!
For that reason some painters copy Bruegel's paintings.
The numerous pictures that were painted in the style of Pieter Bruegel
the Elder after his death, made the art of the great
Master known throughout the centuries.

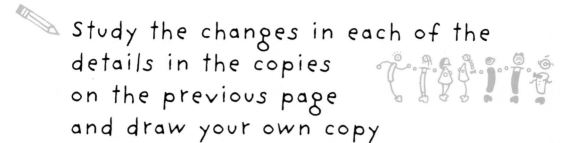

Study the changes in each of the
details in the copies
on the previous page
and draw your own copy

Texts and illustrations: Catherine de Duve
Research: Catherine de Duve and Lucie Hanquet
Graphic design: La Page

Photography:
Brussels:
© Royal Library Albert I, Print collection:
Portrait of Pieter Bruegel the Elder, in Dominicus
Lampsonius, 1572: p.4
The Alchemist, Philippe Galle after Pieter Bruegel the
Elder (ensemble and details), around 1558: p. 10, p. 11
© The Royal Museums of Fine Arts of Belgium:
Pieter Bruegel the Elder
The Census at Bethlehem (details), 1566: cover, p. 18,p. 19, p. 25, p. 30
The Fall of the Rebel Angels (details), 1562: cover, p. 24
The Fall of Icarus (ensemble and detail), around 1555-1560: p. 2, p. 8, p. 12, p. 13
The Adoration of the Kings (details), around 1555-1557: p. 3
Winter Landscape with Skaters and Bird Trap, 1565: p. 26-27
Pieter Brueghel II
The Fight between Carnival and Lent (details): p. 20, p. 2, p. 24, p. 25
The Wedding Dance in the Open Air (details), 1607: p. 24, p. 25
Flemish Fair (details): p. 28
after Jan Brueghel I
Bouquet of Flowers (details): p. 29
Rembrandt
Portrait of Nicolaas van Bambeeck (detail), around 1640: p. 25

Vienna:
©Kunsthistorisches Museum
Pieter Bruegel the Elder
The Tower of Babel (ensemble and details), 1563: p. 2, p. 4, p. 5
Children's Games (ensemble and details), 1560: cover, p. 16-17, p. 18, p. 19
Peasant Wedding (ensemble and details), around 1568: p. 22, p. 23, p. 24, p. 25

Berlin:
Pieter Bruegel the Elder
© Staatliche Museen, Gemäldegalerie
The Flemish Proverbs (details), 1559: p. 14, p. 15, p. 24

With thanks to: Éliane De Wilde, chief curator of the Royal Museums of Fine
Arts of Belgium and to the educational service, to Brigitte de Patoul, Thérèse
Marlier, Sabine van Sprang, Rik Snauwaert and Mélanie Berghmans and to all
the people who contributed to the realization of this book.

www.kateart.com